What Are You Wearing?

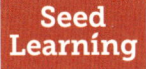

hat

coat

scarf

T-shirt

skirt

shorts

pants

boots

What are you wearing?

I'm wearing a hat.

What are you wearing?

I'm wearing a T-shirt.

What are you wearing?

I'm wearing a scarf.

What are you wearing?

I'm wearing boots.

What are you wearing?

I'm wearing pants.

What are you wearing?

I'm wearing a coat.

Let's learn more about Indonesia.

Nasi Goreng